Waves

Karishma Gomez

ISBN: 978-0-646-73712-6

DEDICATION

To my mum, my friend, my partner -
We live this life together.

Then. Now. Always.

Dear Reader,

This collection is more than a journey through loss or a cathartic exhale - it is a love letter, to the greatest love of my life.

We all express love using different tools; I have chosen words. Much like love itself, I have found they can be powerful and everlasting - whether written, spoken, or shown.

If these words resonate, I hope they make you feel seen and offer you a sense of comfort and strength.

With love and thanks,
Karishma x

INTERTWINED

You say I love you,
I say I love you more...

Because loving you is breathing,
It's simply all I know

It's a bond that spans a thousand stars
And fires a thousand more

Intertwined like your hand in mine,
No matter where you soar

And yet, *tu me manques*,
Until we meet once more.

OUT OF REACH

You're just out of reach,
And I can't comprehend it

My calls won't go through,
My messages left unread

And yet I can speak to you,
Inside of my head

But I won't hear your voice,
Or your beautiful laugh

The best sounds I know -
Gone, in a blink and a half.

GRIEF

(Inspired by 'A Grief Observed', by C.S. Lewis)

I've read countless words,
On how this all feels
Hoping understanding,
Will help me start to heal

Because comprehension is rare,
Amidst the ordeal

One did resonate, above all the rest -
So much so, it put my pen to the test

It was an idea by C.S. Lewis -
Where in losing you,
I lost your part of me...

The part reserved for you,
The one only you see
The child within -
The softest I'll ever be.

COMPLAINT

I have a complaint,
But nowhere to leave it

No office to visit,
Or letter to write

A simple complaint,
Of an early departure

One that has left me -
Ruptured by plight

And I'm sure they'll tell me,
"We all have our season"

And to be grateful,
For our treasured time

But they don't understand,
That I'm lost without reason

And I'm hanging by a string -
The string of my rhymes.

UNTETHERED

I'm out of orbit -
My tether, torn at its seams

The picture is hazy
But the memories, they gleam

The voices are garbled -
Walking a nightmare,
Type of dream

Can a floating singularity,
Be a functioning team...?

THE QUESTION

"How are you", they ask
"How do you expect me to be?" -
Is *not* what I say,
As they stare, expectantly

I know it's asked with love,
So, it feels wrong to dismiss it
But it tends to trip me up,
Each time I reassess it

So enough, of the thoughtful contemplation,
I'm yearning for the blasé automation...

So, I guess, slowly but surely,
I'll edge my way back
And I'll learn to be comfortable,
Trekking this new track.

POLARISING

It creeps up on me -
The weight of this reality
Knowing there's no hope of you,
Simply sitting next to me...

And all your favourite things,
Have become mine too
As I cling on to embers,
Which still waft of you

Some bring comfort,
While others bring pain
There's no rhyme or reason,
Why they don't all feel the same.

ECHOES

There are echoes of you,
In every room
And memories of us,
Constantly in bloom

I don't know how to feel this -
Or how to let it go
Time nor tide can heal this,
And I'm stuck, left in limbo.

FILTERED

Life has lost its lustre,
Since you left it behind

You met it with such muster,
Some of which, I'm trying to find

My rose-coloured glasses,
Now carry a cool-toned hue

It's filtering the world around me,
And tinted my cerulean sky, a steely blue.

POUR

I've lost a whole lifetime,
Of all that could have been
I can see it in my head -
But it'll never be seen

It's not okay -
And time will not heal
I'm floundering in a fate,
Already sealed

Drowning in love,
With nowhere to pour
Left wondering,
Where does it go?

MASCARA RUNS

I look in the mirror,
As I dab on a soft blush

Colours feel abhorrent -
But I'm ghostly without this flush

Almost there, I tell myself
Mascara wand in hand

But it feels like lead, as I twirl
Readying me for my unnecessary plans

Finally done, I look up -
And I'm uncomfortable to find

That despite it all,
I can still look, perfectly fine.

SIEVE

Life passes through me,
A sieve of a soul

Nothing really settles,
Except fool's gold

The veil of the worlds whisper,
As I stumble through the dark

An eerie recognition,
Of my debilitating mark

The hollow is deafening,
When I choose to tune in

So, I work the art of distraction -
And I call it a win.

CHRISTMAS WITH YOU

Christmas looks different
To what it used to be
Like, for example -
The lack of the 7-foot tree

The one you used to put up -
A twig at a time
While singing along,
To our favourite Christmas rhymes

Come Christmas Eve,
And we're dressed in our best
Onwards to midnight mass,
It was how we started the fest

And afterwards,
I remember how you would say -
"Look up, Santa's on his way"

And I still do, each and every day
Except now it's to see you -
Amidst the stars where you stay...

Christmas morning -
Always brought surprises and glee
But I knew, the best gifts,
Were standing right next to me

Continued...

CHRISTMAS WITH YOU contd.

And even through the storm,
That broke us in two
You held us together,
Your love got us through

You preserved Christmas,
In all the ways you could
And further enriched,
A beautiful childhood

Whether it be Christmas,
Or any other holiday
The magic you made,
Is what will always stay
And is what holds me close -
From then, to this day.

THE ART OF DISTRACTION

The chapter always ends,
The credits always roll

Goodbyes are always said,
With "see you laters", oversold

The fights get fought -
Some you win, some you lose

But neither shifts the outcome,
Of the one you didn't choose

They say it's all temporary -
But that's not really true

If life is our permanence,
Some stings throb, the whole way through.

GLIMMERS

I try to sit in gratitude,
Not always easy to do -
Like when you're ending a year,
Which took much more than its due

And yet, I won't discount
The glimmers, if you will...
The joy, the love, the laughter -
The warmth amongst the chill

And if we're talking glimmers,
There are some that come to mind
The stars that shine around me,
Bringing light where there's none to find

So, I'll try to sit in gratitude -
And keep the hollow at bay
I'll fill it with the magic of memory,
Until I reach our 'one day'.

REARVIEW

It's unsettling to know,
The story of us
Sits forever defined
No more permutations,
Only the extrapolations in my mind

I can't look ahead comfortably,
So, I'll switch to rearview
And at each stop I make,
We'll share a glass or two

I can't share my days,
But on the ones that are repetitive
I can go back and find,
A response that is competitive

And with each pour we make,
I'll soon come to find
Each moment has swelled,
With this little love of mine

And if you happen to see,
A tear run down my face
Just know it's evolved from sadness,
It's love in all its grace.

CHEMISTRY

Emotion has drained me,
And left me for dead
I'm struggling to fill,
The gaps in my head

But I'm only human -
Or so they once said
So maybe, just maybe
That will get me out of bed

I'll use adrenaline to fuel,
And serotonin to calm
I'll hit up dopamine to invigorate,
And endorphins as balm

Moods will waft over,
And emotions won't click
But chemistry is science,
And with it I'll stick.

COLLECTION

I saw the perfect cheesecake,
It was at our favourite place

If only I could get it for you,
And revel in the joy on your face

I stare silently at the display,
Playing exactly what you would say...

As I collect another moment,
I can't share with you today.

THE RIVER OF US

The river of us -
No beginning or end
The current overthrows,
Each and every bend

The river of us -
The seas can't comprehend
We cross them and yet
Never merge, only blend

The sands of time,
They were building a fort
We saw it in our path,
And were waiting on a moat

We reached its banks,
Too soon for its tools
And watched our river settle,
As we started to pool

And now our waters glisten,
As they hit the light
A reminder of the river,
In all its might.

SOMETHING BORROWED

If you're feeling shattered
And scattered,
Merely rubble on the floor

Battered and bruised
Till you're numb to the core

And you feel like your light
Doesn't shine anymore...

Here's a reminder of what I now know,
Light doesn't only shine from within,

It can be borrowed from love,
And all you find it in...

ABOUT THE AUTHOR

Karishma Gomez is a creative writer based in Sydney, Australia. She has always been enthralled by the magic of storytelling and is grateful to wield some of it through her Skribbles.

Her previous works include her debut collection, "Skribbles by K" (available on Amazon). She also publishes her ongoing work across her social media profiles under 'skribblesbyk'.

Those close to her would agree, she is known to interject mid-conversation with, "There's a poem in there".

www.ingramcontent.com/pod-product-compliance
Lightning Source LLC
LaVergne TN
LVHW051021080826
845145LV00009B/2746